# Looney Tunes
# MAGIC EYE

## 3D Illusions by N.E. Thing Enterprises

**Andrews and McMeel**

A Universal Press Syndicate Company

**Kansas City**

Published by Andrews and McMeel, a Universal Press Syndicate Company, 4900 Main Street, Kansas City, Missouri  64112.

ISBN: 0-8362-7053-3

Attention: Magic Eye Fans!!

Now you can "see" **Magic Eye** on the web!! View our page at: http://www.magiceye.com

Visit our web page for: sample images for your viewing pleasure, information about our latest books and products, or the scoop behind free viewing and this amazing technology! You can even get instructions on how to see 3D or how to join our fan club!

And please, e-mail us with your questions and comments at: magiceye@tiac.net

Any nonsurfers can U.S.-mail us at:

N.E. Thing Enterprises
19C Crosby Dr.
Bedford, MA 01730

Happy Viewing!

# INTRODUCTION

Feast your magic eyes on *dis*, Doc—the very first *Looney Tunes MAGIC EYE* book. You know—one o' them optical confusion things. The people at N.E. Thing (brother!) asked me to write an introduction, but I don't know what to say (I know—"say N.E. Thing"; ya don't say). Look, I don't need to get my carrots in a bunch and wax effusatative about our cartoons here at Warner Bros.: they're the best. Period. Capital *P*.

Oh, yeah, I could bump my gums till Buster Crabbe Day about "high standards" and "innovative tech-a-nical creativity" and "best-loved images," but, ehhhh—it's a MAGIC EYE book. It's cute. It's a gimmick. Let us not confuse it with endin' world hunger or changin' the course o' mighty rivers or somethin'. Sheesh. It's a *book*. You'll like it. It'll punch up your day, or getcha in good with a friend. Or give ya MAGIC EYE strain.

Whaddya waitin' for? Buy it. It's magic, Doc. Ya can't explain it to somebody. Ya gotta show 'em.

Bugs Bunny
Burbank, California
May 1995


I distinctly remember the editor saying over the phone that the deadline for this introduction was Thursday. Well, **today's** Thursday and everybody and his Uncle Chester says the deadline was last *Tuesday*. Has there been some miscommunication, or am I nuts? Whose introduction got *printed*? And just *how* did that editor get my unlisted number, anyway? WILL SOMEBODY PLEASE TELL ME WHAT'S GOING ON AROUND HERE?

Daffy Duck
Toluca Lake, California
May 1995


Ya forgot, ah say, forgot to mention who put together this here project in the first place! Where'd we be without those N.E. Thingers Tom Baccei or Cheri Smith? Or Bill Clark and Andy (Paraskevas, that is)? And who, ah say, who could forget Ron Labbe? Whattya, all gettin' soft, ah say, soft-headed? These are the *easy* questions, son! Cat got your tongue? And what about Allen Helbig at Warner Bros. Worldwide Publishing—he had a hand in this, too. Helbig, hand. Helping hand! That's a joke son! I'm puttin' 'em in the strike zone but y'not swingin'! What, ah say, what gives?

Foghorn Leghorn
Encino, California
May 1995

# VIEWING TECHNIQUES

Learning to use your MAGIC EYE is a bit like learning to ride a bicycle. Once you get it, it gets easier and easier. If possible, try to learn to use your MAGIC EYE in a quiet, meditative time and place. It is difficult for most people to first experience deep vision while otherwise preoccupied in the distracting pinball machine of life. While others teach you, or watch as you try, you're likely to feel foolish and suffer from performance anxiety. Although MAGIC EYE is great fun at work and other entertaining social situations, those are not often the best places to learn. If you don't get it in two or three minutes, wait until another, quieter time. And, if it's hard for you, remember, the brain fairy did not skip your pillow. For most people, it's a real effort to figure out how to use the MAGIC EYE. Almost all of them tell us the effort was well worth it!

In all of the images in MAGIC EYE, you'll note a repeating pattern. In order to "see" a MAGIC EYE picture, two things must happen. First, you must get one eye to look at a point in the image, while the other eye looks at the same point in the next pattern. Second, you must hold your eyes in that position long enough for the marvelous structures in your brain to decode the 3D information that has been coded into the repeating patterns by our computer programs.

There are two methods of viewing our 3D images: crossing your eyes and diverging your eyes. Crossing your eyes occurs when you aim your eyes at a point between your eyes and an image; diverging your eyes occurs when your eyes are aimed at a point beyond the image.

All of our pictures are designed to be seen by diverging the eyes. It is also possible to see them with the cross-eyed method, but all the depth information comes out backward! Once you learn one method, try the other. It's fun, but most people do better with one or the other. We think that most people prefer the diverging method. Another common occurrence is to diverge the eyes twice as far as is needed to see the image. In this case, a weird, more complex version of the intended object is seen.

One last note before you start. Although this technique is safe, and even potentially helpful to your eyes, don't overdo it! Straining will not help, and could cause you to feel uncomfortable. That is not the way to proceed. The key is to relax and let the image come to you.

## METHOD ONE

Hold the image so that it touches your nose. Let the eyes relax, and stare vacantly off into space, as if looking through the image. Relax and become comfortable with the idea of observing the image, without looking at it. When you are relaxed and not crossing your eyes, move the page slowly away from your face. Perhaps an inch every two or three seconds. Keep looking through the page. Stop at a comfortable reading distance and keep staring. The most discipline is needed when something starts to "come in," because at that moment you'll instinctively try to look at the page rather than looking through it. If you look at it, start again.

## METHOD TWO

The cover of this book is shiny; hold it in such a way that you can identify a reflection. For example, hold it under an overhead lamp so that it catches its light. Simply look at the object you see reflected, and continue to stare at it with a fixed gaze. After several seconds, you'll perceive depth, followed by the 3D image, which will develop almost like an instant photo!

The last pages of this book provide a key that shows the 3D picture that you'll see when you find and train your MAGIC EYE.

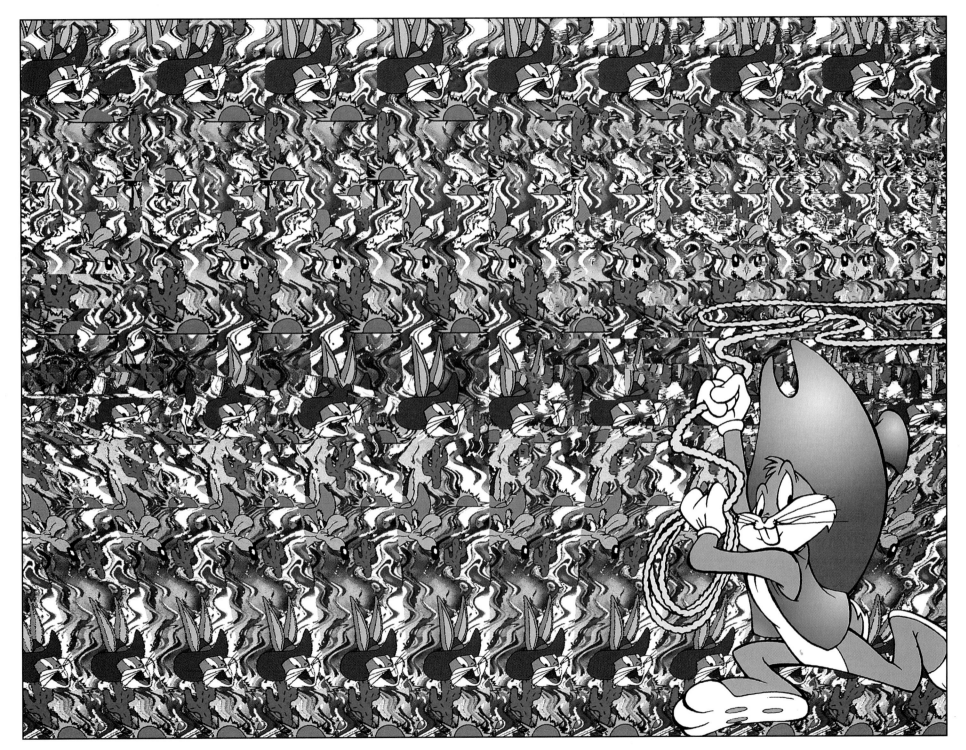

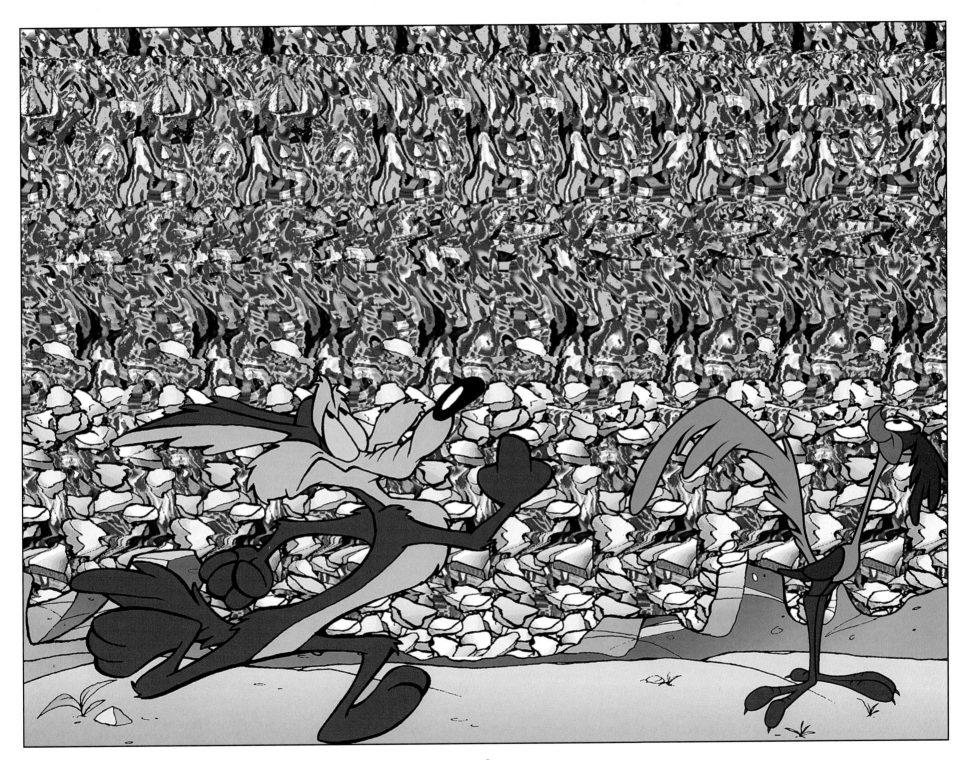

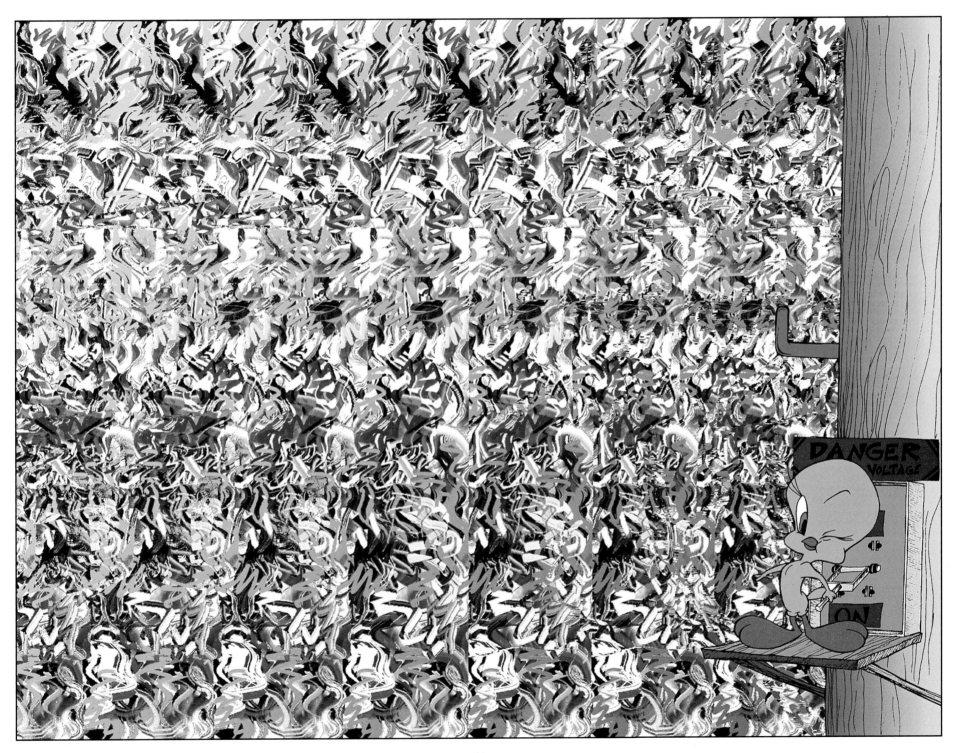

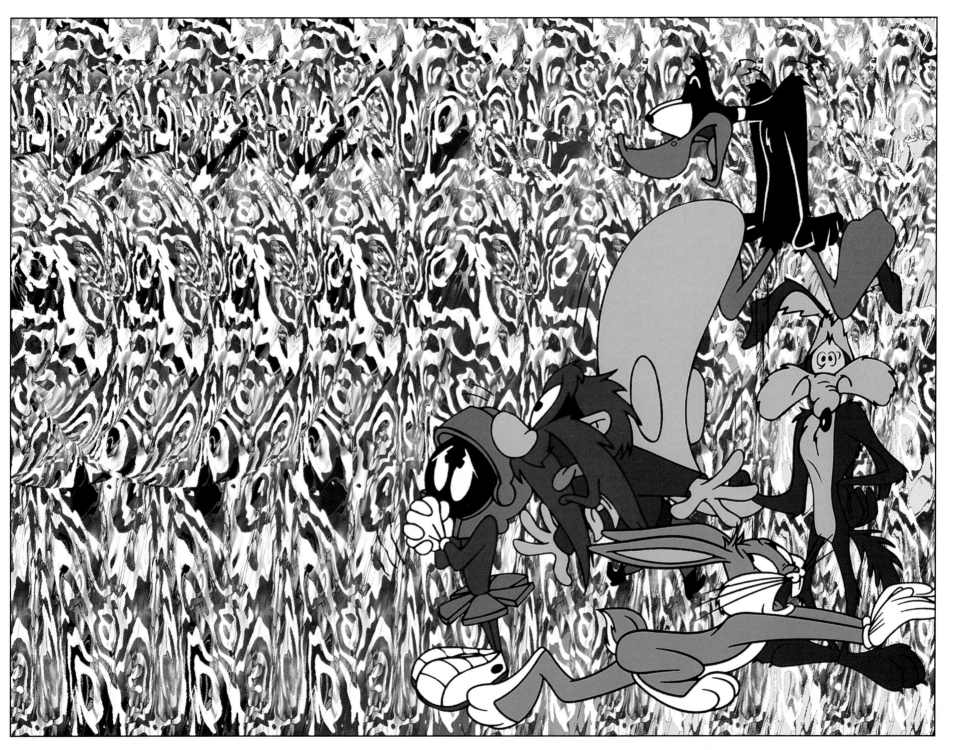

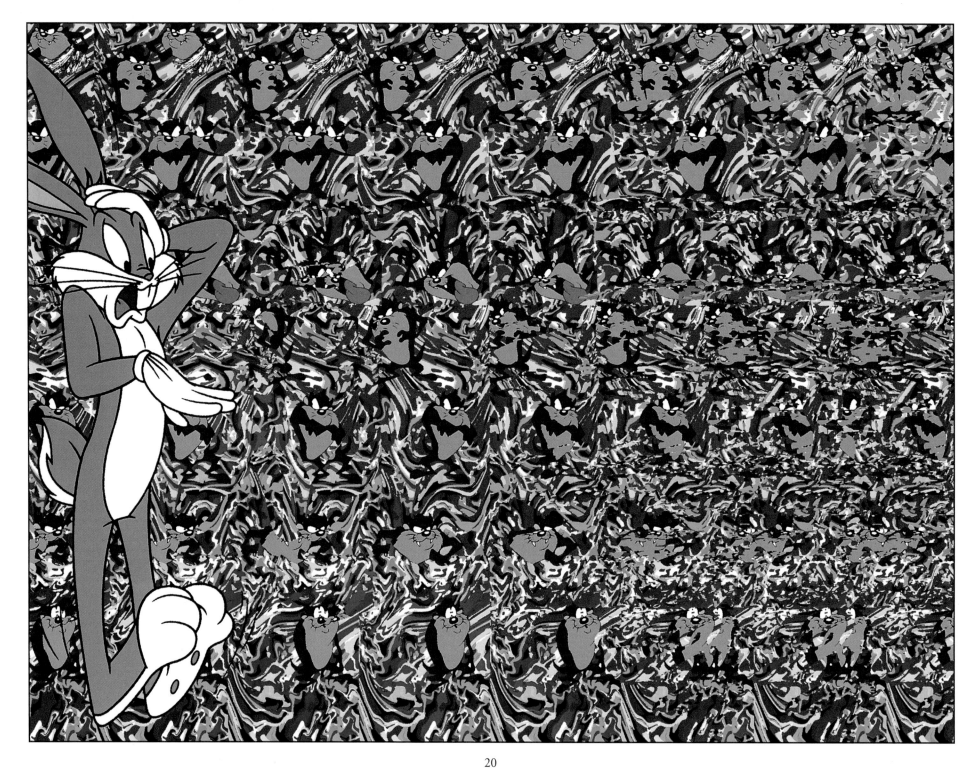

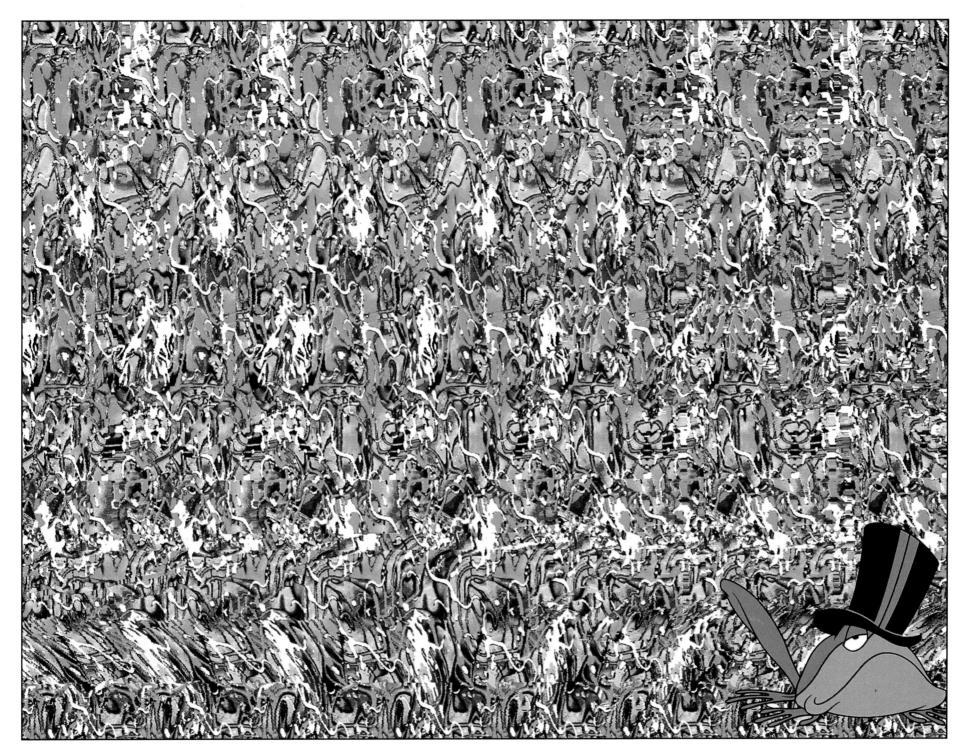

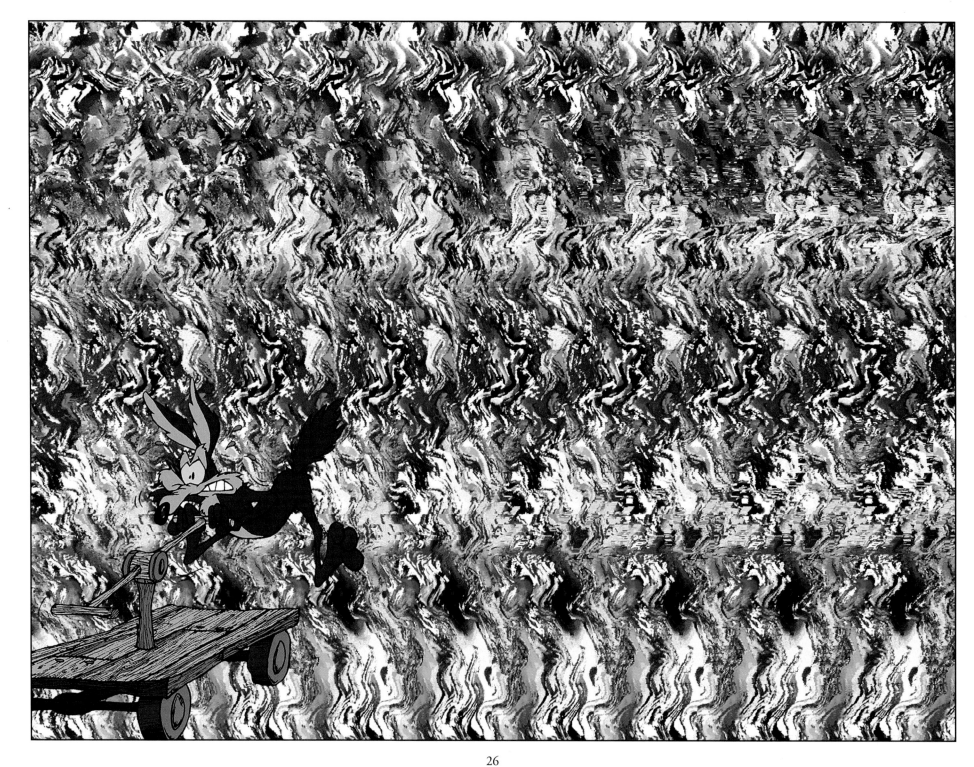

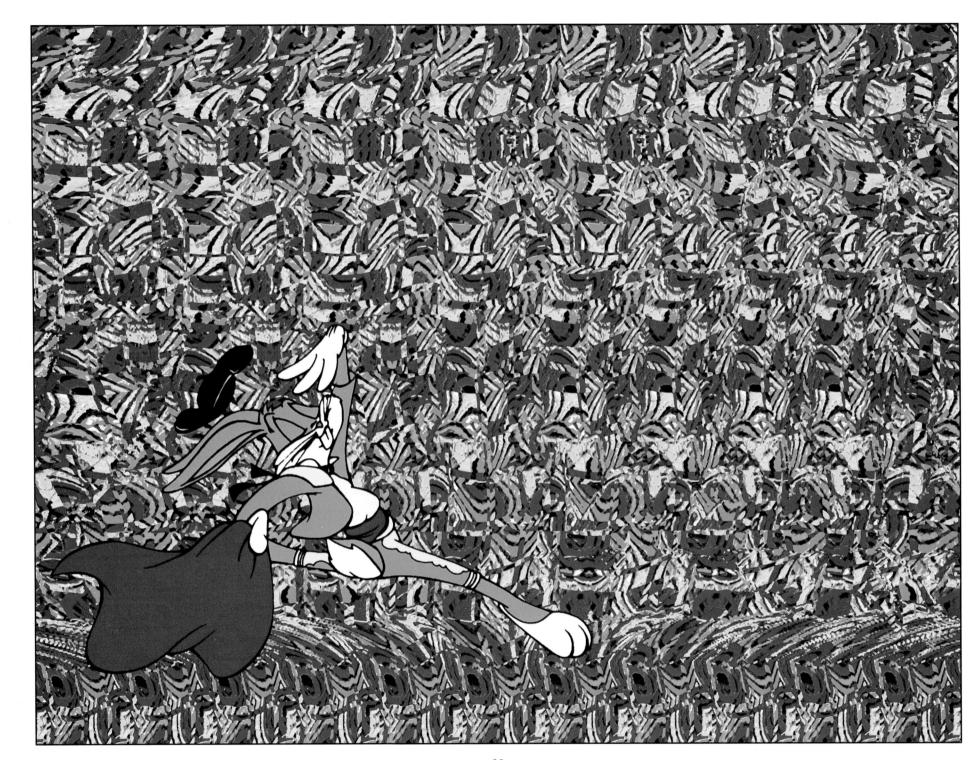

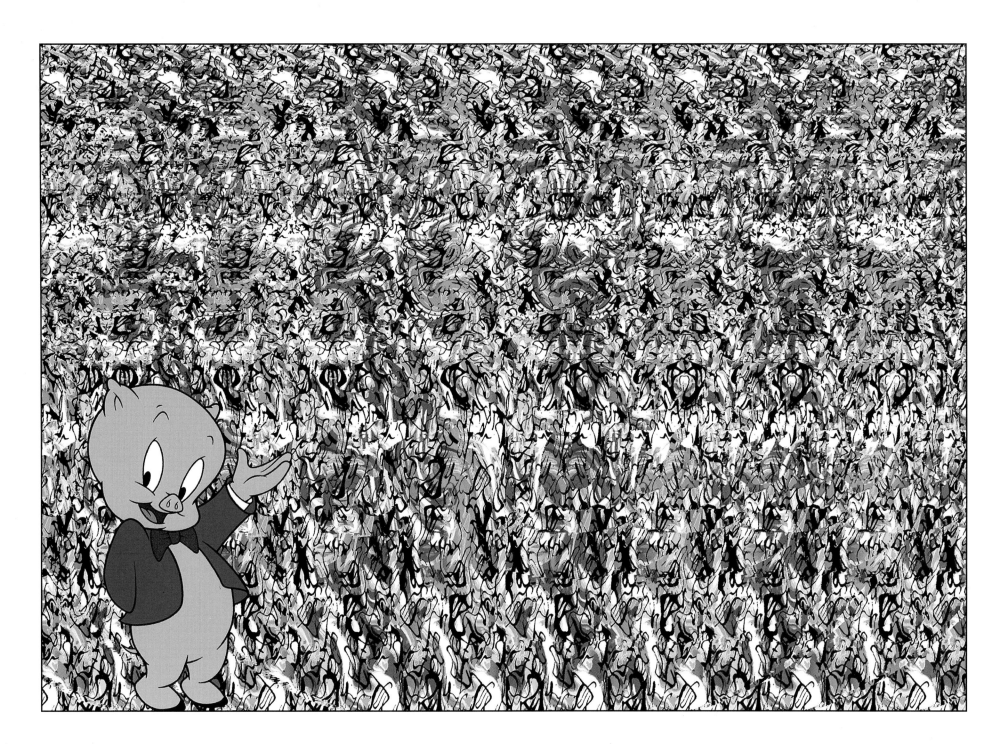

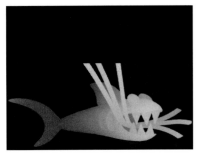

Page 5  Shark

Page 6  Dynamite

Page 7  Stallion

Page 8  Expletive

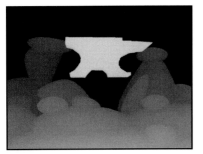

Page 9  Anvil

Page 10  Junk Food

Page 11  Zap Cat
Page 12 (No Image)

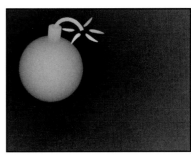

Page 13  Cherry Bomb

Page 14  Piano

Page 15  Heart

Page 16  Reclining Hare

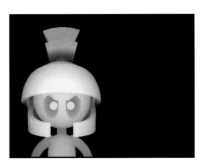

Page 17  Marvin

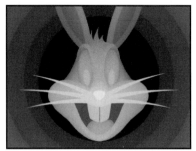

Page 18  Head of Hare

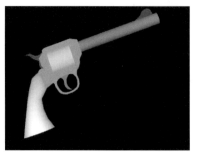

Page 19  Pistol

Page 20  Taz-spin

Page 21  Speedy

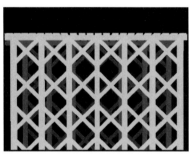

Page 22  Trestle

Page 23  Wile E. Parasol
Page 24 (No Image)

Page 25  Michigan

Page 26  Train Surprise

Page 27  Lab Shelf

Page 28  Steer

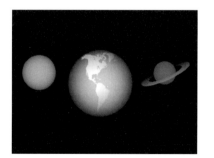

Page 29  Earth

Page 30  T.A.F.

32

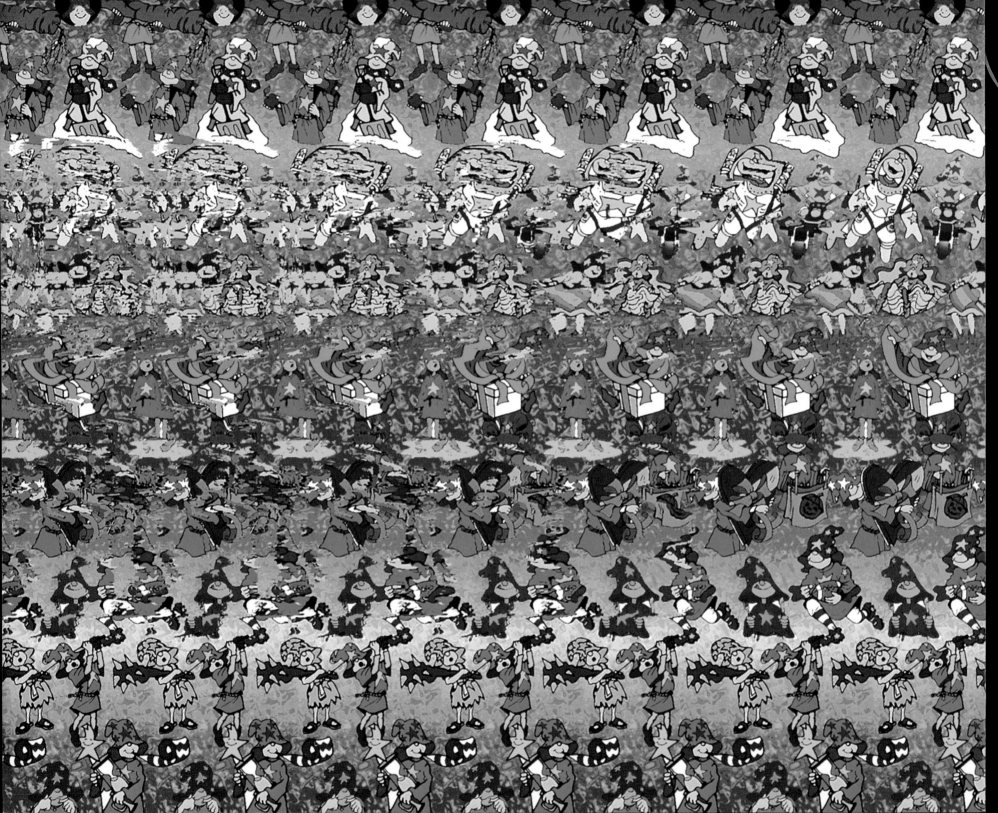